EVERYMAN

VOL. 1
BE THE PEOPLE

WRITTEN BY
THE BROTHERS GOLDMAN

ILLUSTRATED BY
JOE BUCCO

EDITED BY LESLIE AUGENBRAUN

PUBLICATION DESIGN BY
THEREISNODESIGN

ALL CORRESPONDENCE TO
EVERYMAN@ONELOVE.US

PUBLISHED BY FWDBOOKS
ISBN#0-9759152-0-7
PRINTED IN CANADA
FIRST EDITION OCTOBER 2004

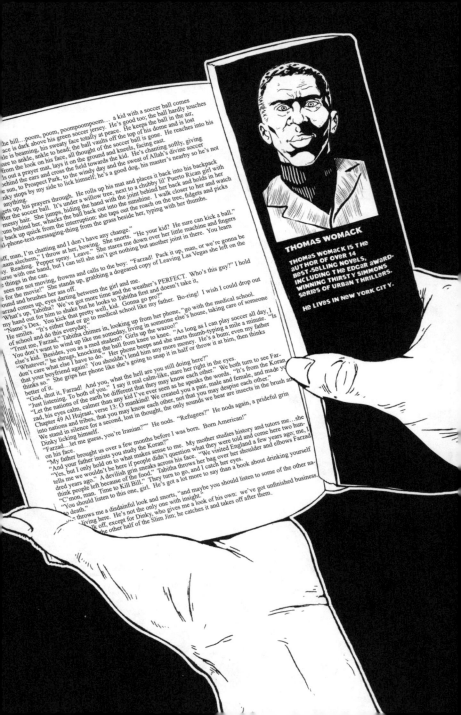

the hill…poom, poom, poompoompoom… a kid with a soccer ball comes
ace is dark above his green soccer jersey. He's good too; the ball hardly touches
le is beaming, his sweaty face totally at peace. He keeps the ball in the air,
nee to ankle, ankle to head; all thought of the soccer ball is gone. He reaches into his
ls out a prayer mat, lays it on the ground and kneels, facing east.
behind the ears and cross the field towards the kid. He's chanting softly, giving
the sun, to Prospect Park, to the windy day and the sweat of Allah's divine soccer
nky stops by my side to lick himself; he's a good dog, his master's nearby so he's not
anything.
gets up, his prayers through. He rolls up his mat and places it back into his backpack
fter the soccer ball. It's under a willow tree, next to a chubby lil' Puerto Rican girl with
messy hair. She jumps, hiding the hand with the joint behind her back and holds in her
runs behind her, whacks the ball back out into the sunshine. I walk closer to her and watch
back up quick from the interruption: she taps out the roach on the tree, fidgets and picks
al-phone-text-messaging-thing from the grass beside her, typing with her thumbs.

off, man, I'm chatting and I don't have any change."
aam alechem," I throw at her, bowing. "Leave." She snorts. "He your kid? He sure can kick a ball."
y. Reading. Pepper spray. Leave." She stares me down over her little machine and fingers
urse with one hand, but I can tell she ain't got nothing but another joint in there. You learn
things in the can.
sees me not moving, frowns and calls to the boy: "Farzad! Pack it up, man, or we're gonna be
ound and brushes her ass off.
for the movie!" She stands up, grabbing a dogeared copy of Leaving Las Vegas. "Who's this guy?" I hold
arzad comes up, eyes darting between the girl and me.
What's up, Tabitha?" We've got more time and the weather's PERFECT.
"Name's Dex. You kick that pretty well, kid. Gonna go pro?"
my hand out for him to shake but he looks to Tabitha first and doesn't take it,
"Trust me, Farzad," Tabitha chimes in, looking up from her phone, "go with the medical school.
You don't want to wind up like me someday, giving in someone else's house, taking care of someone
else's kid. Besides, you as a med student? Girls up the wazoo!"
"Whatever," he shrugs, knocking the ball from knee to knee. "As long as I can play soccer all day, I
don't care what else I have to do." Her phone beeps and she starts thumb-typing a mile a minute. "Is
that your boyfriend again? You shouldn't lend him any more money. He's a bum; even my father
thinks so." She grips her phone like she's going to snap it in half or throw it at him, then thinks
better of it.
"God, shut it, Farzad! And you, what the hell are you still doing here?" I say it real calm-like, stare her right in the eyes.
"Just listening. To both of you." I say I've ever seen as he speaks the words. "It's from the Koran
zad, his eyes calm, calmer than any kid I've ever seen as he speaks the words. "It's from the Koran
"Let the nations of the earth be different that they may know each other." We both turn to see Far-
Chapter 49 Al Hujraat, verse 13: O mankind! We created you a pair, male and female, and made yo
into nations and tribes, that you may know each other, not that you may despise each other."
We stand in silence for a second, lost in thought, the only sounds we hear are insects in the brush an
Dinky licking himself.
"Farzad…let me guess, you're Iranian?" He nods. "Refugees?" He nods again, a prideful grin
on his face.
"My father brought us over a few months before I was born. Born American!"
"And your father insists you study the Koran?"
"Yes, but I only hold on to what makes sense to me. My mother studies history and tutors me…she
tells me we wouldn't be here if people didn't question what they were told and come here two hundred years ago." A devilish grin sneaks across his face. "We visited England a few years ago; me, I
think people left because of the food." Tabitha throws her bag over her shoulder and elbows Farzad
"C'mon, man. Time to Kill Bill." They turn to go, and I catch her eyes.
"You should listen to this one, girl. He's got a lot more to say than a book about drinking yourself
o death."
s throws me a disdainful look and snorts, "and maybe you should listen to some of the other na-
living here. He's not the only one with insight."
lk off, except for Dinky, who gives me a look of his own: we've got unfinished business.
he other half of the Slim Jim; he catches it and takes off after them.

THOMAS WOMACK

THOMAS WOMACK IS THE AUTHOR OF OVER 14 BEST-SELLING NOVELS, INCLUDING THE EDGAR AWARD-WINNING THIRSTY SIMMONS SERIES OF URBAN THRILLERS.

HE LIVES IN NEW YORK CITY.

MISSION STATEMENT
ONLINE LEGISLATION LAB
WORKS IN PROGRESS
ARCHITECTS
GET INVOLVED

CLICK

APRIL 27, 2004
2227 F STREET, WASHINGTON DC

ONELOVE.US   MISSION STATEMENT

OneLove is a political movement dedicated to restoring common decency to government, along with a respect for its citizens, by promoting programs designed to unify the country person by person. America is not, and has never been, a welfare state; the history of the United States is told through the struggles of its people to better themselves and carve out their own niches in life. In keeping with that history, OneLove puts its policy emphasis on the PEOPLE and the freedoms Americans have strived to maintain for themselves. The economic proposals OneLove offers are designed not to simply allow the government to take care of its people, but to EMPOWER Americans to earn a living, find their calling, and give this country an internal strength and pride not seen since the New Deal and WWII.

Respect yourself. Get involved. ◄ **CLICK**

NEW MESSAGE TO INFO@ONELOVE.US

Sir/Madam:

My name is Manolo Perez and I am currently President Birch's personal aide. As such, I have see and hear things you do not; serving this administration is a very different experience than the last… there are things happening here you already know, but behind these walls, I can get you the proof. I believe in the America of my dreams; it's not so far away. I want to sign up. Someone has to do something. Contact me via this anonymous remailer.

Manolo Perez|

TOKITOK-TOK-TOKITOKITOK-TOKITOK-TOK

"WORD TO YA MOMS/I CAME TA DROP BOMBS--"

"--I GOTS MORE RHYMES/THAN THE BIBLE GOT PSALMS..."

HOW YOU FEELIN' THIS MORNING, *PREZ*...?

I'M FEELING LIKE I *FELL ASLEEP* AT MY DESK AND *DREAMT* I LIVED SOMEWHERE *DOWNTOWN*.

JOIN THE CLUB, SIR. MY *BLOOD T* IS CURRENTLY *MILK THREE SUGARS*.

MISTER PRESIDENT, THERE'S A CELEBRATION FOR KEVIN STOCK'S *PROMOTION* GOING ON IN THE *MURAL ROOM*...

MISTER VICE PRESIDENT THOUGHT YOU MIGHT LIKE TO SAY A FEW WORDS OF *INSPIRATION*...?

OH, FOR CHRISSAKES... THROWING KEVIN A NEW *TITLE* AND A BLONDE ASSISTANT TO TAKE HIS *DICTATION* IS ALL THE INSPIRATION THAT LITTLE *WORM*'LL NEED.

MANNY, TELL THE VICE PRESIDENT I'LL BE THERE IF THERE'S *COOKIES*.

ACTUALLY, SEND HIM *HERE*. I'LL TELL HIM MYSELF.

THEN GO GET YOURSELF SOME *COFFEE*. YOU LOOK LIKE *WARMED-OVER SHIT*.

GOOD BOY.

--CALLS FOR A *DRINK*, HENRY. THOSE TECHIE BOYS IN GEORGIA HAVE SEWN IT UP FOR US THIS TIME WITH THESE *VOTING MACHINES*.

NO MUCKING AROUND WITH *PAPER BALLOTS* AND *JUDGES' RULINGS*.

IF WE COULD HAVE DONE THE SAME FOR *MY DADDY*, WHEN HE WENT TO BAT FOR *RE-ELECTION*...

AFTER HE LOST... YOU'VE NEVER SEEN SUCH A *MIGHTY* MAN BROUGHT SO *LOW*. HE HAD A HUNDRED JOB OFFERS IN THE PRIVATE SECTOR, BUT HE WOULDN'T HEAR *ANY* OF IT.

AHHHH... BUT NOW, WE HAVE THE POWER TO *STA[Y] ON COURSE.*

IT'S A *WONDERFUL THING* FOR US, HENRY, IF WE KEEP OUR EYES -- AND PRESS'S -- ON *THE FUTUR[E]* NOT THE PAST.

FOUR MORE YEARS... WE CAN BE BACK IN AFGHANISTAN BEFORE THE INAUGURATION, HAVE THE SPECIAL FORCES BOYS CLEAN HOUSE, WAVE *OSAMA'S* PICTURE AROUND--

--AND HAVE THAT *NATURAL GAS PIPELINE* OPERATIONAL FOR THE FOLLOWING *CHRISTMAS*.

WE'RE THE *SHAPERS* OF THE *NEW AMERICAN FUTURE*, HENRY. YOUR FATHER WOULD BE PROUD AS HELL, WERE HE STILL WITH US.

AMERICA REJECTED HIM... AND IT BROKE HIS HEART.

Handcount Systems CONFIDENTIAL

EVERY DAY, WE'RE *REINFORCING* THE PILLARS THAT HOLD THIS NATION *ABOVE THE MUCK*:

OUR MORAL FIBER, OUR BUSINESSES AND THEIR GOVERNMENT CONTRACTS, PERCEPTION THAT AMERICA... *UNBEATABLE*.

TWO MONTHS LATER

FUH MIHRUN DUHRUHS??

6:39PM THAT NIGHT EAST VILLAGE, NYC

NO, *FOUR MILLION DOL-LARS.* IT'LL BE A FEW DAYS UNTIL THE WIRE TRANSFER'S SET UP.

SO I GUESS IT'S *FRIES FOR EVERYO* ON YOU, HUH, ELVIS?

AND HOWEVER MUCH *MS. PAC-MAN* TWENTY BUCKS CAN BUY!

SO WHAT DOES THIS MEAN? WHAT'RE YOU GOING TO DO WITH ALL THAT *MONEY?*

OOH....!

FIRST, I'M GONNA DRAG YOU OFF INTO THE PARK AND *KISS* THE HELL OUT OF YOU...

DITA, I'M A *PUBLICIST*. I PLAY FOR KEEPS AND I PLAY TO MAKE PEOPLE'S DREAMS A *REALITY*.

OOH. HOLD THAT THOUGHT, MACK. *THIS* OUGHTA BE *GOOD*. TALK TO YOU IN *TEN*.

FILL OUT THOSE FORMS, AND YOU'VE GIVEN ME *ANOTHER* CARD TO PLAY ON YOUR BEHALF, ON YOUR DREAMS' BEHALF... IF IT COMES TO THAT.

THEN LET ME ADD A NEW WRINKLE... WHAT DO YOU THINK ABOUT *THIS* PLAN B?

Caller ID Blocked

AL! HOW'S MY LITTLE *HEADCOUNTER* TODAY?

MAN, *SHUT UP*, KARL! JEEZ! THE *WALLS* HAVE *EARS*!

YOU, UH, YOU GOT MY *DEAL* LINED UP?

WELLLLLL, SUBJECT TO *VERIFICATION*, OF COURSE, AND ASSUMING YOU DON'T NEED A *GHOST-WRITER*... YEAH. RANDOM HOUSE WILL GUARANTEE A *$100K ADVANCE* FOR YOUR STORY.

AND ROYALTIES?

FROM: schase@rhouse.com
Karl—
This would be a helluva coup, but you better check this guy out before you even try to make him an offer. The Bigs will cut ties with you if something like this turns out to be bogus after they've signed a check.
Let me know?
xoxo, Sarah

THEY'RE STANDARD... LOOK, AL, YOU'RE NO *BOB WOODWARD*. YOU'RE JUST A GUY... IN THE RIGHT PLACE TO WRITE A *MONUMENTAL EXPOSE*.

THE BOOK'LL DO GREAT AFTER THE *ELECTION* AND IT'LL BE *TRASHED* BY THE CONSERVATIVE PRESS BY THE INAUGURATION, ASSUMING HE WINS. NOW WHAT DO YOU *HAVE* FOR ME?

AUGUST 6, 2004, 5:53PM
THE WHITE HOUSE

OH, NO.

AAAAAAAAHHH!!

THEY *SHOT* THAT GUY!

WHAT THE HELL IS THE *MATTER* WITH YOU PEOPLE?

--*TAKE* THOSE GUNS *AWAY* FROM YOU--

YOU WON'T RESPECT OUR *VOTES*, WE WON'T RESPECT YOUR *ORDERS*

--JUST WANTED TO KNOW *WHY*

ER, ONE VOTE! ONE VOTER, ONE VOTE! ONE VOTER, ONE VOTE! ONE VOTER, ONE VOTE! ONE VOT
ER, ONE VOTE! ONE VOTER, ONE VOTE! ONE VOTER, ONE VOTE! ONE VOTER, ONE VOTE! ONE VOT

--GIVE US THOSE--

GODDAMN IT, LET GO! DAVE, GARY, CALL FOR BACKUP!

WANT TO KEEP US DOWN

HEY, THEY'RE JUST DOING THEIR JOBS

SHUT JERK...

ER, ONE VOTE! ONE VOTER, ONE VOTE! ONE VOTER, ONE VOTE! ONE VOTER, ONE VOTE! ONE VOT
ER, ONE VOTE! ONE VOTER, ONE VOTE! ONE VOTER, ONE VOTE! ONE VOTER, ONE VOTE! ONE VOT

THIS WAS THE START OF WHAT MEDIA SOURCES ARE NOW REFERRING TO AS THE ELECTION RIOT.

THOUSANDS OF ARRESTS, TENS OF THOUSANDS OF INJURIES, SEVENTY-FIVE FATALITIES INCLUDING SIXTEEN POLICE OFFICERS, PROPERTY DAMAGE SCATTERED ALL ACROSS DOWNTOWN, AND PROTESTORS ARE STILL FINDING THEIR WAY BACK HOME.

NEWS-4 ELECTION RIOT

PRESIDENT BIRCH WILL BE RETURNING TO WASHINGTON AS SOON AS THE NATIONAL GUARD AND LOCAL AUTHORITIES CAN GUARANTEE HIM *SAFE PASSAGE*...

NEWS-4 ELECTION RIOT

HEY, DON'T BOTHER KILLING THE MESSAGE... WE'LL DO IT FOR YOU!

DES MOINES INT'L AIRPOR
FOUR DAYS LATER

THE CAPITOL BUILDING
INAUGURATION CEREMONY

CAN YOU SMELL THAT IN THE AIR, MANNY? THIS IS GOING TO BE THE TERM THAT MAKES HISTORY; THE LAST ONE WAS JUST THE BEGINNING.

YESSIR, MISTER PRESIDENT.

MY NAME IS MANOLO SANTIAGO PEREZ, AND I'VE BEEN THE AFFIRMATIVE-ACTION PERSONAL AIDE FOR PRESIDENTS CLINTON AND BIRCH OVER THE LAST 6 YEARS. I'VE GOT SOMETHING TO SAY TO YOU PEOPLE WHILE THE CAMERAS ARE ALL POINTED UP HERE, TELL YOU WHY THIS UNION SHOULDN'T GO FORWARD... BEFORE DEATH DO US PART. I HAVE TO, SOMEONE HAS TO SPEAK OUT BEFORE WE ALL MAKE A HUGE MISTAKE FOR THE SECOND TIME: SWEARING IN THIS MAN TO RUN THE COUNTRY.

PRESIDENT BIRCH **STOLE** THIS ELECTION. HEADCOUNT RECORDS LEAKED TO THE PUBLIC **CONFIRMED** IT. **4 MILLION AMERICANS** CAME OUT AND PROTESTED IN THIS CITY ALONE AND THEY WERE SMACKED DOWN LIKE THEY WERE **BEGGING FOR CHANGE** ON CAPITOL HILL.

EVER SINCE, PEOPLE HAVE BEEN **SIMMERING**, KEEPIN' QUIET, POWERLESS. SO I AND PEOPLE LIKE ME PLANNED THIS, ONE LAST GAMBLE, ONE LAST PLEA FOR SANITY. WE COULDN'T SHAME THIS MAN OUT OF OFFICE... AFTER ALL, HE STILL CLAIMS HE WON THE ELECTION **FAIR AND SQUARE!**

AND SO ENDS AN AFTERNOON THAT WILL RING OUT IN AMERICAN HISTORY; EXACTLY HOW IT'S REMEMBERED... THAT DEPENDS STRONGLY ON THE NEXT 72 HOURS.

LILLI HIGGINS, LIVE FROM WHITE HOUSE LAWN

MEANWHILE, KARL PERKINS, SPOKESMAN FOR THE ONELOVE CANDIDATES, HAS RELEASED EXTENSIVE BIOGRAPHIES ON WOMACK AND OROZCO...

AS WELL AS A PLATFORM STATEMENT THAT MIRRORS MANY OF THE PROPOSALS LISTED ON ONELOVE'S ORIGINAL WEBSITE.

HIGHLIGHTS INCLUDE A MINIMUM-WAGE HIKE WITH A COMPREHENSIVE TAX CREDIT PACKAGE FOR SMALL BUSINESSES, A ROLLBACK IN THE TAX CUTS FOR THE TOP BRACKETS...

... THEIR OWN EDUCATIONAL PACKAGE INCLUDING PLANS FOR CHARTER SCHO⟨OL⟩ BASED ON THE MONTESSORI MODEL.

...AND AN UNUSUAL PROGRAM CALLED EVERYMAN, DESIGNED TO PROMOTE TRANSPARENCY IN GOVERNMENT, AMONG OTHERS.

THE WHITE HOUSE STILL HAS WOMACK AND OROZCO IN PROTECTIVE CUSTODY...

BUT BOTH CANDIDATES HAVE BEEN ALLOWED TO CONDUCT PHONE INTERVIEWS FROM THEIR CELLS.

HEY, WE HADDA PRESIDENT WHO WAS AN ACTOR AND THAT WASN'T TOO BAD....WHY NOT A WRITER?

I THINK WE OWE IT TO OURSELVES TO GIVE THEM A CHANCE. THAT MR. BERRY, HE'S A POLITICIAN, NOT A LEADER. AND PRESIDENT BIRCH... HELL NO!

I'D VOTE FOR MR. WOMACK ANY DAY OF THE WEEK.

SHE THINKS HE'S FIII-IIIINE!

OF COURSE WE DON'T KNOW THEM. WE DON'T KNOW ANY PRESIDE⟨NT⟩ OR VICE-PRESIDENT THAT WELL WHEN THEY'RE ELE⟨CTED⟩ BUT YOU GO ON WHAT YOU'RE GIVEN, AND ⟨I⟩ LIKE WHAT I SEE.